A Stroke

A SOLDIER'S JOURNEY

ALVIS E. SMITH

WESTBOW
PRESS®
A DIVISION OF THOMAS NELSON
& ZONDERVAN

This book is a work of non-fiction. Unless otherwise noted, the author
and the publisher make no explicit guarantees as to the accuracy of
the information contained in this book and in some cases, names of
people and places have been altered to protect their privacy.

WestBow Press books may be ordered through booksellers or by contacting:

WestBow Press
A Division of Thomas Nelson & Zondervan
1663 Liberty Drive
Bloomington, IN 47403
www.westbowpress.com
844-714-3454

Because of the dynamic nature of the Internet, any web addresses or
links contained in this book may have changed since publication and
may no longer be valid. The views expressed in this work are solely those
of the author and do not necessarily reflect the views of the publisher,
and the publisher hereby disclaims any responsibility for them.

Any people depicted in stock imagery provided by Getty Images are
models, and such images are being used for illustrative purposes only.
Certain stock imagery © Getty Images.

Scripture quotations are taken from the New King James Version. Copyright
© 1982 by Thomas Nelson, Inc. Used by permission. All rights reserved.

ISBN: 979-8-3850-2600-5 (sc)
ISBN: 979-8-3850-2601-2 (e)

Library of Congress Control Number: 2024910491

Print information available on the last page.

WestBow Press rev. date: 07/10/2024

Contents

Dedication

In loving memory of my grandmother, Mrs. Eliza Smith, my mother, Mrs. Mary McQueen, and my aunt, Mrs. Mamie Edwards. They all passed away and left a part of themselves within me. I hope that I have exercised their gifts throughout my life, for each shaped me into the man I am now today. They instilled in me the importance of believing in God, the bond of family, and the benefit of building strong relationships with others.

Acknowledgement

This book represents a culmination of dedication and hard work during the past three years, starting with my lovely wife, Deana - she was my advocate. She took me to all of my medical appointments; she made sure that everything that needed to be addressed was set up in my apartment to support my effective healthcare. She also made sure that I had the right doctors for my after-care.

I also want to pay my gratitude to my medical team of doctors, nurses, therapists, and personal trainers, as they all ensured that my medications and therapy were in alignment with my progress, and were perfectly administered.

Thank you to Dr. Abdou, my primary medical doctor at Burke Inpatient Rehabilitation Hospital, who coordinated all of my in-patient care plans when I arrived, after being discharged from White Plains Hospital.

Thank you to all of the Burke Inpatient Rehabilitation Hospital therapy team who made my stay and care possible. Thank you to the host of out-patient Burke Rehabilitation care providers who helped me tremendously with my post-discharge care plan. Thank you to the visiting caregivers and other in-home healthcare providers who were a tremendous and supportive team, and helped me gain confidence in rebuilding my self-esteem and skills.

Thank you to Dr. Susan Soeiro and all of the caregivers within the White Plains Physicians Associates. The many specialists who were put in my pathway and supported me by giving vital and supportive medical care, and guidance to restore my health. Thank you to Dr. Soeiro for putting me in contact with Dr. Amy Hua – Neurologist Supreme!

I am eternally grateful to all who took their time for my care and support. Without these committed medical professionals, I know that I would not be the person who I am today. I'd like to thank my Better Homes & Garden Rand Realty family for all of their support, care, and concern. I appreciate all that you did to support me during this critical time in my life. I am eternally grateful to you. I am thankful for all you have done for me.

Foreword

To all those who have had health and wellness struggles and ended up on a wayward path:

> *Be kind to yourself on this road. There will be no shortcuts.*

Your journey towards healing will have its ups and downs, with many opportunities to meet people as they are. Some will join you for a short walk, some will be there only at the finish line, and some will lend a hand to tackle obstacles along the entire way. If you are fortunate to have someone by your side, may the healing power of relationships light your way toward wellness. Those meaningful connections surpass anything that modern medicine or procedures alone could ever replace.

You are not alone. Dig deep, and be courageous enough to keep moving forward. You'll find opportunities for support where you least expect it.

To Al and Deana:

When I first joined you on your journey of stroke rehabilitation, you were overwhelmed with treatment options, medications, complications, and physical and mental restrictions, all of which weighed heavily on you as you struggled to put one foot in front of another. I remember when you grieved the ability to put your pants and shoes on while standing or be able to drive by yourself.

Medically, you were supported by the best rehab team, doctors, and therapists, but more importantly, you had Deana's unwavering support, which has been an anchor in your journey to wellness.

As the months and years rolled on, you progressed from being stuck in a wheelchair to walking with a cane to walking on your own two feet again. I was thrilled to see you regaining your independence in self-care. Never have I been as excited as I was to hear you recount cooking an entire dinner for you and Deana to enjoy.

It has been an honor to walk with you on your journey, Al.

Amy Theresa Hua, DO

Chapter One

A STROKE OF LIFE

A creative train of thought is set off by the unexpected,
the unknown, the accidental, the disorderly, the
absurd, and the impossible.

—Asger Jorn

L ife takes us through unexpected turns. It challenges us with
everything we know about ourselves and the world around us.
It doesn't announce its arrival; it barges in uninvited, reshapes
reality, and yields difficulties that sometimes demand us to tap into
our undiscovered strength.

Undiscovered strength – reminds me of the story of Ash Fisher.
A writer and comedian based in Oakland, whose life turned upside
down when a chronic illness took over. She called the experience "the
door to my life slammed closed." In other words, you may describe
it as one day when you're normal, and then suddenly, you're sick.
She was emotionally trapped in a dark place, where her journey was
dotted around with multiple misdiagnoses, and she was eventually
forced to let go of her dreams. She fell into depression, and her illness
suffocated her through constant pain.

My story unearths a similar experience. It reminds me of the resilience I carried within my journey. Every heartbeat foretold a tale of struggle since the day my world shifted. The sudden and mysterious breakdown came like a ball of fire in the sky, casting shadows that overlapped the impending storm. Little did I know that within all those moments of glee and little tales of downsides, my life was about to take a turn I could never have anticipated.

Days turned into weeks and weeks into months. I almost felt like each step, echoed the thud of uncertainty. It was a symphony of discomfort, a rhythm that overpowered the strength of my heartbeat. Despite my attempts to drown it out with the clamor of daily routines, the pain persisted. I didn't realize the sickness would appear as an unwelcomed guest in my life that overstayed its welcome.

As I was tossed around amongst an army of whitecoats, the air carried the weight of countless stories of my own brother's suffering and his life-altering circumstances. Doctors became my confidantes, their eyes reflecting a mixture of empathy and clinical detachment. Medical tests became a routine, a ritual I participated in with the hope that each result would be the key to unlocking the mystery of my condition.

Eventually, my mind unleashed a torrent of questions that cascaded through it like an unbridled waterfall. I asked myself, *how does one navigate a life reshaped by physical limitations? Would my illness define me? Would I become a mere reflection of the restrictions imposed by my body?* The questions lingered, casting a pall over my thoughts. I was unaware of what happens when the body becomes a battleground, and when every day is a skirmish for survival. I searched for these answers but they slipped through my fingers like grains of sand. With the weight of uncertainty, I grappled with a burden that grew heavier each day. The disconnection between the mind and body is palpable as they surrender control. With this lack of control over my body, I placed my faith in the hands of strangers providing me medical care.

Since the day I succumbed to my illness, the journey ahead was daunting, a path fraught with challenges that took me to an ambiguous territory. It was definitely a journey into the unknown and a pilgrimage of self-discovery. My story is not just a survival legend but a testament to the indomitable human spirit. As the pages unfold, you will walk with me through the valleys of despair, scale the peaks of triumph, and navigate the unpredictable terrain of living with a chronic illness.

There even came a time when my body was exposed to the height of the pandemic. Medical professionals surrounded me, dressed in protective gear. I was isolated due to COVID precautions, being trapped and examined like a specimen. I struggled with the loss of privacy, particularly in matters of personal care, which is highlighted. In the midst of this struggle, I discovered a paradox — the more I resisted these shadows, the more power they seemed to wield over me. Only when I acknowledged their presence did I find the strength to move forward. Acceptance became my compass as it guided me through a daunting sickness.

Amidst the trials, I encountered unexpected allies — fellow travelers in my miserable realm. This was where I learned the importance of faith, prayer, and the support of loved ones in navigating through a difficult journey. Their stories resonated with mine. In our shared experiences and the isolation of illness, I found community. We became a lifeline for each other – we didn't just share the burden of symptoms but also those small triumphs.

Relationships underwent a metamorphosis. Friends became pillars of support; they shared their empathy and became a balm for the invisible wounds to the naked eye. My family, especially my wife, became steadfast allies in the battle for normalcy. There was no denying that the shifting dynamics seemed overwhelming to them, but we forged bonds that transcended the physical body's limitations.

> "Fear not, for I am with you; Be not dismayed, for I
> am your God. I will strengthen you, Yes, I will help
> you, I will uphold you with My righteous right hand.."
>
> —*Isaiah 41:10 New King James Version*

I delve into this verse, and it just makes me realize how living with a prolonged illness can evoke fear and anxiety about the uncertainties of the future. I recall its impact on my daily life and the many challenges that came with it. This part of the verse reminds me that God's presence is a constant source of reassurance while facing illness. It invites us to release our fears, allowing us to find comfort in knowing that we are not walking this difficult path alone.

Prolonged illness can be emotionally and mentally draining. It can cause rampant discouragement and, in a sense, illness forges a personal relationship between the individual and God. It encourages those facing illness to find solace in the fact that, despite the difficulties, they are known and cared for by their Creator. The relationship taps into our inner strength and resilience. This promise from God imprinted in this verse affirms that divine power is available to sustain individuals through the challenges of their illness. The assurance of God's help suggests that there is support beyond human capabilities.

In short, this is a story of adaptation. It is about the recalibration of dreams, rewriting expectations, and accepting a new normal. As you toggle through my account, you'll discover that normalcy is not a fixed point but a fluid state of being. It is found in the laughter that echoes through the pain and in the love that shatters through the confinements of a weakened body. And in the simple pleasures that become monumental victories.

As you navigate through these words, you will join me in unraveling the layers of existence where challenges accompany each heartbeat of mine. Welcome to my world, where strokes aren't just strokes of misfortune; they are strokes of life, shaping a narrative that defies the boundaries of adversity.

Chapter Two

LIVING LIFE

M anaging real estate offices in the Bronx and Yonkers, I led an active life in a seven-day-a-week industry at a time when the business was beginning an upswing. It was a bloodbath happening in our market; the Bronx and Yonkers had brokers and agents having their hands dipped deep inside the market. It was difficult to stand out in your business alongside these giants. Client acquisition was the hardest part. Running a real estate business in that area meant dealing with clients that were demanding, unreasonable, and unrealistic. Oftentimes, it was stressful enough to pull our hair out of our scalps. If you're one of those pawns or vanguard of that market, a nine-to-five job was just another myth for you. You were destined to handle high-pressure, skull-crushing situations to satisfy your clients.

I thrived on learning the market and grooved on keeping the pace back and forth between both offices. I served on community boards that had local residents, business owners, and community leaders in their portfolios. It helped me to tap into the neighborhood's dynamics. In return, they'd offer me feedback and input on my development plans. It was quite helpful to anticipate concerns and issues before any brawler started knocking on my door.

5

Even on Sundays, I would personally take a drive-by to check out open houses to keep current on the prime properties available. After having spent too much time in this industry, I got to know a thing or two in that landscape. You always need to have your head in the game. Waking up, staying up late, going out, you take your business everywhere you go. You could never anticipate when you might make that home run, but your routine, habits, and relationships were definitely going to take you there. I intended to build relationships with competing realtors to recruit them into one of my offices. And honestly, I was really good at it.

Tuesday mornings started extra early with a run for breakfast treats to serve up at our weekly informational and motivational sales team meeting. The realtors I supported were the secret sauce to the success of the agency. We'd gather in a large meeting room to commune, share best practices, face challenges as a team, and break bread together. I considered many of them my friends and worked long hours to lend support and help close the real estate deals.

People running businesses often underestimate networking. There is so much to get from those pep talks in boardrooms and fancy dinners. Time is the real currency in business, and it all depends on where you spend it. One of the reasons I understood the game so quickly was by spending my time at the right places. Even when I was socializing, cashing in on my leisure hours, I was building relationships with my clients. Hands-on, I was getting referrals from mortgage brokers, real estate attorneys, and home inspectors. Even our community events didn't stop us from mining access to off-market opportunities. If you get your hands on real estate deals not featured in the market, it would be appropriate to assume that you have a certain competitive edge over others.

Serving as an usher at Living Word Christian Church in White Plains, I'd travel from the Bronx office to attend Saturday evening services. Wednesday night was my Bible study class. There is very little that could stand in the way of my commitment to serve my church and cultivate my faith in God.

Living Word Christian Church, non-denominational and multi-cultural, was my spiritual nourishment. There was no other place more welcoming and uplifting, allowing everyone there the chance to find their sense of purpose. The experience was majorly dissimilar to what you would see in traditional churches that catered to a specific audience. They allowed everyone to open their mind to a variety of subjects; each individual was set off to explore their own spiritual path without judgment or restriction. The teachings mainly allowed me to focus on personal growth, trying to awaken my inner self and uncover that hidden potential. Our spiritual nourishment takes place beyond the confinements of Sunday church service. Take, for example, community outreach: serving the underprivileged and downtrodden ignites a spirit of compassion and empathy. Church taught me that the journey to finding one's sense of purpose was not solitary but a shared expedition.

In my youth, growing up in the South, I'd be the first of nine siblings to awaken to the smell of mom's pancakes or my stepdad's homemade biscuits every Sunday morning. While my mom did most of the cooking and kept us well-fed, there was something decadent about the biscuits, often doctored with bacon, grits, or eggs and cheese.

Sundays were special for us, and as the oldest, I supported our morning rituals by wrangling my siblings out of bed, directing them into their best clothes and shoes, hair grooming, and tooth brushing to become presentable for the congregation and in reverence to Our Lord. It was usually the same clothes every week, but sometimes appearing on a different kid. Four boys and five girls, we were close in age and shared what we had. Once dressed, we'd stream into the kitchen around our oversized rustic wood table with varying degrees of wakefulness.

The table we'd surrounded as a family for years living in Montgomery, Alabama, was scarred with unintended rings and subtle carvings of numbers and letters that bled through the paper from hours of collective homework. Flecks of paint and glitter embedded in the table's wax further captured our family's unique art and history.

After full-bellies, we'd load into our wood-paneled white and brown station wagon with stepdad driving us about five miles to enter the large double doors of the old, cared-for red brick Baptist church that hosted one large room and more people than it could hold. With our community of fellow followers who would rise up unified in song, prayer, and praise, I never experienced loneliness as a child. We'd leave the service with renewed adrenaline from the positive energy that coursed through the entire building and spilled out onto the lawn. Other than the adventure we'd find as our own tribe of Smiths playing outdoors, the memories of the Sunday mornings of my youth will be treasured for my lifetime. This helped who I, Alvis Eugene Smith, became as a man.

My adult life in New York included monthly meetings with my Mason fraternity brothers, often running late into the evening with fraternity functions. While "Masons," by definition, construct using stone, blocks, and brick, our focus was not on physical labor but on cultivating and building exemplary lives. The differences we possessed served to unify us through moral, intellectual, and spiritual conversations. We were a community of strong men from diverse religious and spiritual backgrounds, grounded in mutual respect for the unique perspectives we shared. It was enlightening and enriched my view of the world.

Rituals reserved just for me provided a weekly reset with peace and purpose to find respite from the fatigue of my chaotic pace.

At the end of a long week, my mentor and colleague, Clayton Jeffrey and I would meet up for a happy hour on occasion. Working together in real estate, we became fast friends. Like-minded, we didn't compete. Instead, we'd throw creative ideas around and uplift each other to succeed as an unstoppable, formidable pair in New York's real estate market. Weekends brought backyard barbeques with our wives. Clayton's the kind of friend I enjoyed seeing every day. When the day came that all changed, our friendship morphed with the change. The energy of sitting across the table became less dimensional, seeing and talking from screen to screen, with the only interruption being the demise of our Wi-Fi connection. Our friendship and commitment to have each other's back remained as solid as ever.

When serving in the military, I picked up boxing as an adrenaline and fitness boost. You might term it as a high-intensity cardiovascular exercise practiced through a combination of aerobic and anaerobic exercises. It is also a type of full-body workout. Boxing activates a lot of muscles in the process; all those punches, footwork, and defensive movements really take your anatomy to the next level.

By nature, I'm calm and gentle. Therefore, I was only interested in winning, not inflicting pain. To achieve that, you needed to work on your feet and head movement, work on delivering punches through a controlled force instead of swinging wildly, and mainly target the body without causing excessive trauma.

Moreover, sparring with my military brothers meant there was an unspoken respect to not cause injury that could derail their service to the platoon. By nature of my size, as I built strength and technique, I became known as a daunting opponent. I had surprisingly an excellent stance, balance, and mobility when I entered the ring. They described me as unpredictable since I used to break down different jabs, crosses, hooks, and uppercuts.

Older and a bit arthritic, boxing became a hobby at the gym down the street from the Bronx office when I could find an hour to exercise.

I was unknowingly wearing myself down with a mediocre diet, trying to do it all, and not getting enough sleep. The real estate upswing was short-lived when we all experienced a global punch in the face. The emergence of the pandemic. It was a forceful swing and knockout. All of us were finding ways to regain our footing.

At the beginning of the unpredictable pandemic in March 2020, we were trying to keep real estate moving and had to pivot fast. I had no choice but to shut down both offices and find ways to support my realtors to creatively sell without direct human contact. Home buying is personal. It's about walking through a house and using your senses to determine if it's a place that could ultimately be called Home. It's tactile. The hustle of selling real estate is hard enough. Imagine it without the ability to explore communities, neighborhoods, and properties sitting beside an interested client.

My world was crashing all around me in the pandemic. The market became volatile and shattered the confidence of buyers. It was painful to see many of my prospects putting their plans on hold. Realtors had to eventually adapt to virtual showings and online meetings. Remote work was the new norm, and the challenge that came with it was the business cost. To sum it up, if not for the pandemic, we wouldn't have learned the true potential of technology for our businesses.

My COVID-era job became anticipating the resources realtors would need to do their jobs remotely while remaining successful. Prior to the pandemic, we didn't want people shopping online for their dream home. In the new COVID-world, online technology and humans had to partner closely to buy and sell properties. One could not survive without the other. An invisible heavy cloud with a steel lining of stress became overwhelming. We all contended with too many unknown factors.

Though there was a sudden sense of isolation, I found strength in knowing I wasn't the only one adjusting. Like a daily ticker, the number of people getting sick, being admitted to the hospital, and dying couldn't be stopped until COVID was clearly defined and scientists could find the best solution in hopes of resetting the world back to its non-pandemic state of a month earlier. I took it all seriously. Life could be worse if I got the virus.

My person, my partner, my wife, my Deana lived in Arizona. When I was offered the chance to run large-scale real estate offices in New York, Deana and I decided together that it was a career-building opportunity I really couldn't refuse. Over the years, her professional growth has been impressive working for the NCAA (National Collegiate Athletic Association), NFL (National Football League), and then ASU (Arizona State University), Sun Devil Athletics. Her career path was every bit as important as the chance I was being offered. Building new connections and finding her purpose at ASU meant she couldn't leave the Phoenix area and the comfort of our two-story stucco home on a cul-de-sac, with a lake framed with palms and surrounded by a walking path. Together, we committed to commuting cross country for a couple of years.

We had a shared vision for our future, with geography being the only thing that separated us. We talked and had evening video calls to confide and share the events of the day. We weren't under the same roof but remained stable in support of one another. In the scope of our lifetime, living apart for a couple of years seemed manageable before we'd re-evaluate our careers and locations.

In retrospect, I see now that I had such a focus on keeping up a chaotic pace in my day-to-day life. I lost sight of what should have been my number one priority - my own health. It wasn't until my body malfunctioned that I realized standing at the sink to turn on the faucet for a drink of water was something I never really thought of and totally took for granted. It had never occurred to me that one moment could change everything - including something as simple as getting a drink from only a few feet away but completely beyond my reach.

Chapter Three

BEING HUMAN

W hen "it" happened, I didn't really know what happened. On an early Sunday morning in April, just a month after the COVID lockdown happened, I walked into the den and turned on the television for the daily pandemic updates. It was customary for people stuck in lockdowns at that time to have their televisions fired up early morning, getting all the latest up to date headlines about the pandemic. The pandemic was the only thing I thought posed the biggest threat to my work, livelihood, and health.

Tossing the remote on the couch, I turned to walk back toward my bedroom to retrieve my Bible for my morning scripture reading ritual. A few steps in, I clumsily fell hard over a box between the den and the kitchen. Pain shot up my left thigh as I banged my knee on the hardwood floor. Scraped, bleeding, and throbbing, I laid there on the floor for a long minute, evaluating if I was all right before attempting to pull myself to my feet; I felt wrong. It was more than my injured knee. The strength and control I had moments before drained from my left arm, down through my leg, like some unfamiliar invisible force had attached itself to me and was pulling energy from my limbs. I could move everything. I wasn't paralyzed.

But my whole left side was weak, and I felt disconnected from the workings of my brain.

I completely lacked the control and ability to lift myself. As I continued to try to stand, I grew tired and exasperated. My confusion over the sudden failure of my body escalated to fear that something bad, really bad, had infiltrated and possessed me.

With my phone perched on the bedside table, it might as well have been a hundred miles away. There was no way of getting to it. I tried to scoot on my right side but couldn't make any progress forward with my tall, muscular frame. I realized even if I could get there, I wouldn't be able to reach it anyway.

I rested, thinking maybe this was some kind of temporary episode that would pass. Not knowing how long I'd drifted into sleep when I woke up, my thoughts were foggy and random. I tried to focus and re-acquaint myself with the reasons I was on the floor. The answer was floating and flitting like a hummingbird I couldn't capture.

COVID news with a handful of less important yet noteworthy events recycled for hours until the TV went into reset mode, turning the programming off and leaving behind the tint of a subtle blue screen. My fear was met with despair and loneliness as the sun set and night flooded my apartment. A crack of light appeared under my door to the hallway, and the neon signs from the gas station across the street were slivers that cut through the darkness.

Thoughts of my younger brother, Michael, streamed through my mind like an old-fashioned film strip showing itself on the cream wall in front of me. Michael was ten years younger than me. He was such a smart and quiet kid, very thoughtful. I'd taught him how to drive in his early teens. His interest in the stock market and trading was piqued by the time he was 18. This was the start of his path to a career in finance. It was at the bank he worked, on an ordinary day, that he collapsed.

I tried connecting the dots with what happened to my brother: *Am I experiencing what he experienced? Could this be a stroke?* He was only 50 when it happened to him. It took medical services about an hour to get him to the hospital. I'd been on the cold, hard floor for hours and not getting any better.

The situation was frightening, as much as my thoughts were disoriented. I was confused, facing difficulty in comprehending my surroundings by the time I lost control. My body struggled to coordinate with its limbs, with a sudden loss of balance.

Waves of anxiety and panic nipped at me as I remembered how, by the time Michael was admitted to the emergency room, as a family, we had to make a quick and difficult decision to allow the doctor to make an incision in his skull to relieve swelling around his beautiful, smart brain. If we waited too long, his medical prognosis would likely get worse. It was these thoughts that resonated with me and I knew it was important to seek immediate medical attention at times like these to bring about the best possible outcome. Because some strokes may be preceded by Transient Ischemic Attacks (TIAs) or 'mini-strokes,' they pose as a warning sign that a stroke may occur in the future, in which case, medical attention is necessary.

I learned the hours before the stroke; my brother woke up to his routine – just like me. There was nothing different about his day: Shower, dress, grab a piece of toast, and he headed out the door to his 9-to-5 gig. He couldn't see around the corner to stop the blow that day would deliver.

He survived, but the stroke changed him irreparably. Michael still lives in a rehabilitation facility and is unable to walk or talk. He is predicted to live his remaining years there.

At 60, I couldn't fathom a move into an assisted living community, never to escape and to become completely vulnerable, dependent on others for absolutely every aspect of my personal maintenance. I envisioned a stark reality of potential dependence, where my own identity would be wrapped up in self-sufficiency for, God knows how long, maybe decades. Deana and I had a plan and vision for the next ten, twenty, thirty years together. Travel and enjoy the life and financial freedom we'd both been working so hard to build. My mind was already struggling between the desire for continued independence and recognition of potential limitations. The idea of assisted living became a challenging contemplation, more than an opportunity for adaptation and showing resilience in the face of life's challenging circumstances.

My grandmother also suffered two strokes. She recovered from the first after three weeks in a rehabilitation center and showed steady, persistent improvement. As long as I knew her, through good and bad times, she beamed a positive attitude. You could actually see it in her face. The way she looked at people and sincerely listened. She had a talent for seeing the best in people and bringing it out in them. I genuinely believe her mental strength was pivotal to regaining her quality of life. Through mindful meditation, she visualized her recovery and found a way to connect the strength of her mind to fuel her weakened body.

Thoughts of Grandmother calmed me and gave me hope that whatever was happening to me would get better just like it did for her. I needed to breathe and meditate myself back to the way I was 24 hours earlier. If she could do it, I could also decide to do the same. Many years later, when she turned 93, the last year of Grandmother's life delivered a second stroke, forcing her to spend her remaining days in a rehabilitation facility. Like Michael, unable to walk or speak.

Strokes can be inherited generationally through a combination of various genetic and environmental factors. Families may show certain genetic variation that exposes them to a stroke risk, such as hypertension, cardiovascular diseases, and diabetes. Moreover, a family with a history of strokes is more prone to develop risk factors associated with strokes. For instance, if most family members suffer from issues of high blood pressure or high cholesterol, this represents that their condition is most likely influenced by genetic and lifestyle factors. Maybe that explains more of my family's recurring medical issues involving the same predicament.

The line of light peering under the door to the hallway outside of my apartment cast occasional shadows of feet walking by. My mouth and throat dried and cracked as I tried to be heard. The sound couldn't come loud enough for someone to distinguish my plea for help through the closed and locked door.

Cold, tired, and curled on my side, I drifted in and out of sleep with moments of waking to wonder if this was all a dream. I'd wake to the realization that I couldn't retrieve a warm blanket, pour myself a glass of water, or even make it to the bathroom to relieve the pressure in my bladder. Again, all easy-to-manage functions of everyday life I never considered could be taken away from me. Not a dream but my new reality.

I woke to the sound of the sunrise cleaning crew in the hallway Monday morning and tried to call out. I couldn't hear more than the thoughts in my head and raspy, faintly whispered words.

Having heard the vibration of my phone a few times peppered into the late evening hours, my thoughts went to Deana. I had no doubt my wife had been trying to reach me. I'd missed our family video call that Sunday to get a status on her Mom's COVID hospitalization in Indiana. Navigating her mother's care without being allowed to be at her bedside, I worried about her. It was hard to imagine juggling work responsibilities while her mom was on a ventilator. And now, I was unable to talk to her, let alone offer support and a little comic relief from her stressors. She's a strong, independent, brave woman, but she feels deeply for those she loves. No doubt, her heart was heavy with worry.

When I met Deana, my life forever changed. After having completed two tours in Iraq, I was in the Army Reserves at Fort Benning and a real estate broker in Georgia. Eventually, I was invited to attend and participate in my cousin's son's wedding in Indianapolis, Indiana; my cousin and Deana's mom were friends. The two of them got together and decided it would be good for Deana and me to become each other's date for the wedding a couple of months down the road. Cupid masterminds flitting around the two of us with their little arrows of love potion; our respective phone numbers were shared. A month or so after the flurry of the deployment of their match-making scheme, I received a call from a familiar number – not because I'd called it, but because I'd watched my phone for it to come through. I was intrigued, interested, and hopeful that Deana was all that my cousin promised. By the end of an hour-long conversation, there was a commitment to meet in person at the wedding only a few weeks away, which was locked down.

Unfortunately, the wedding was canceled. Two months later, Deana and I continued talking daily sometimes multiple times a day. Eventually, we found the opportunity to meet in Washington, DC. She was working for the NCAA at the time and she flew in from Indianapolis for a meeting in Philadelphia, Pennsylvania. She arrived shortly before me at Dulles International Airport.

Walking from baggage claim to ground transportation, as I passed through the second door, my heart jumped. After all of this time exchanging emails, texts, letters, and photos, here she was, staring at me from near the curb. Only a couple of inches shorter than me, she wore curve-flattering belted blue jeans, a finely pressed white blouse, and black two-inch pumps. Her eyes brightened, and her radiant ivory smile broadened as I approached Curb 2C, where we'd agreed to meet before picking up the rental car. Her face was flawless and elegant, with dark olive eyes framed by rich, deep brown curly hair. We greeted each other with a long, comfortable embrace as though we'd hugged a hundred times before. Her warmth was disarming; she was more than I'd imagined in person. Not only her looks but over the course of our journey back and forth to Philadelphia, dining, shopping, and then wandering the streets of Georgetown, this long weekend marked the start of a future that was just getting started. I wasn't going to let go of that easily.

My thoughts continued to circle around my wife, my family, my church, and my co-workers. Monday morning, I was supposed to host a team call with a pre-published agenda. That wasn't going to happen. Surely, someone will know that something's wrong. I don't "stand up" anyone, especially the important people in my life.

My left knee ached and stuck to the inside of my gray sweats from the drying blood. Dehydrated and thirsty, the weakness on my left side prevailed. Sleep didn't have its normal restorative powers this time. I felt smaller than my six-foot, two-hundred-pound self. Two days ago, I was able to live my pandemic-era life working from home, exercising in the apartment gym, and carefully planning shopping and take-out food-buying excursions. Now I was alone, vulnerable, and unable to do for myself. The room looked higher and bigger from my newly imposed perspective from the kitchen floor. For the first time in years, I couldn't feel my own size.

I mumbled to myself, trying to figure out how I could get someone to help me as time passed. The more I tried to pull myself up, the more drained I became. If only I could get up in my bed. I didn't want to die alone on a cold wood floor of dehydration and be found that way, an embarrassing final memory to leave behind.

My fear turned to humility as I lay flat on my back, and my mind filled with prayer, *"Lord, please help me. Please give me the physical, mental, and spiritual strength to survive. Lord, please send me somebody."* I knew God was with me and would see me through this, even though I didn't understand why this was happening to me. It happens when an unforeseen calamity falls upon one; they begin questioning the reality, finding the reason, and initiating their search for the rationale that binds them to unwanted circumstances. There had to be a reason. I was grateful to be alive and be given a chance, and I wasn't ready to die. To leave Deana and all we'd planned for our future, I didn't want that cut short. There was still too much to see and do. My will to live overshadowed the despair over my malfunctioning body.

As evening approached, I drifted in and out of sleep. Swallowing became uncomfortable for my dried tongue, sore throat, and cracked, crusty lips. I assessed the value of a sip of water. To me, it would have been liquid gold at that moment. Just a sip.

Once again, as the neon sign from the gas station next door began to replace the fading light in my apartment, there was a startling pounding on my apartment door.

I was startled, in a state of mere consciousness; I moaned and tried to say, "What?" Panicked, I didn't want whoever it was to leave. Someone, feet away, was literally knocking on my front door. My prayers are being answered, and someone is here to check on me.

"Hey Al, you in there? It's Clayton. Deana called me. She's worried about you, man. We all want to make sure you're ok."

I was able to say, *"I can't get up and need some help."*

"What, Al? What'd you say?"

I was able to yelp, *"Help."*

With the help of our building manager, the door opened but was abruptly stopped by the security latch I'd put in place Saturday night before bed. Cracked, I could see a dark, familiar eye. Seeing a fraction of Clayton's face was like being wrapped in warm blankets. Tears filled my eyes with relief that I wouldn't be alone on this floor much longer.

Seconds later, Clayton was talking faster than usual with an edge of anxiety. Not to me, but to summon the rescue squad. Within minutes, the firefighters broke through my latched door, and two masked paramedics knelt beside me. Clayton and others stayed outside, with the police managing curious onlookers by enforcing COVID social distancing and masking protocols.

I was quickly carried down the front stairs of the building and loaded into the ambulance, where we sat for nearly ten more minutes. I saw Clayton out the back window talking to the ambulance driver. He'd instructed him to take me to White Plains Hospital, which was a little further away but known to deliver the highest quality care in the area.

Once Clayton learned that I was stable and in good hands, he called Deana – my hero who knew me and knew I would never go more than 24 hours without hearing the sound of her beautiful voice.

God had delivered on my prayers, restoring my faith in somehow knowing I would be ok.

God is my healer. No matter what my body is telling me, I trust God to heal me and bless me with vibrant health and overflowing joy.

Chapter Four

MY SAVIORS

The connection between my mind and body was severed. I barely remember the trip to the hospital – other than the sound of sirens. Vulnerable, I possessed a different type of gratitude, born of desperation and despair, unlike anything I'd ever felt. *As I lay in that liminal space, battling through consciousness and uncertainty, I eventually realized that I had lost mastery over my own body and decisions; it just slipped through my fingers.* My circumstances demanded a surrender to the unpredictable nature of fate. I found myself in a position where I had no choice but to put my trust in the hands of strangers. I saw their faces blurring in and out of focus as they worked to restore some sense to the chaos that engulfed me at that moment. Soon, my control of my body and ability to make decisions was no longer within my grasp. I had to surrender and have faith in the strangers around me.

Having people touch me, remove my clothing, and inject my body with liquids was all foreign to me. I had to trust them to the depths of the faith I have in God with something as important as my physical well-being. But I feel like I know God, His greatness, His goodness, and His mercy. These people are helping me, and they don't even know me, nor do I know them. *Why do they do this?*

Why do they dedicate their time, hands, and hearts to help a complete stranger? It would be down the road that I would discover the answer to these questions.

A CT scan and the emergency room doctors at White Plains Hospital confirmed my worry about this being a stroke. The sterile hospital environment and the clinical assessments painted a vivid picture for me, not seeing myself in the mirror for nearly 48 hours. I hadn't realized that the left side of my face was drooping. My left hand, arm, and leg were weak and uncoordinated. Each movement was an arduous negotiation between intention and execution. It highlighted the profound impact the stroke had left on my anatomical functions. My knee still hurt from the fall I'd taken in the apartment. Overall, I felt detached from my normal self. These physical limitations led me to be estranged from my normal self. It was as if I were a mere observer of my own existence, navigating through a reality that had become distorted and unfamiliar.

The IV fluids that coursed through my veins gave me a boost of hydration with the sound of heart monitors pinging low tone alarms when my vitals didn't register at acceptable levels. The cuff snugged around my bicep, tightening frequently and interrupting my doze. Medications were given through the IV to lower and stabilize my blood pressure.

I learned through my brother's experience that the more time that passes without treatment for a stroke, the more difficult it is to reverse its long-term impact. Without prompt intervention, the affected brain cells begin to die due to a lack of oxygen and nutrients. The longer this process continues, the more challenging it becomes to reverse the impact. Time is a crucial factor in stroke treatment because certain interventions are most effective when administered as quickly as possible. Such treatments aim to restore blood flow to the brain and minimize the extent of the damage. Hence, instead of minutes or even hours, my delay was for days. This was not a good place to start my dig out from this physical rock bottom.

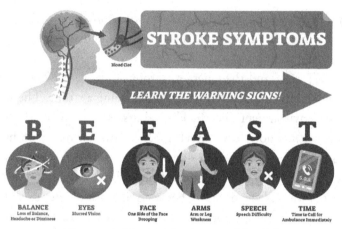

Figure 1: *Physical Symptoms of Stroke*[1]

At the height of the pandemic, it was strange being in the emergency room. Institutional and over-crowded with people all dressed in the same blue gloves and cap, and white masks and disposable jumpsuits - they called '*bunny suits.*' The people caring for me didn't seem recognizable each time they pulled the curtain back. I was in a fog and couldn't see their mouths when they spoke. This annoyed me, as did the fatigue of the bright lights above. I felt trapped, unable to move, and like a specimen in a lab getting hooked to machines. They were all seeing me from the inside out, and I couldn't even see their mouths or noses.

It was in the early days when the Center for Disease Control scientists were still trying to figure out if this rogue, life-threatening strain of the coronavirus could be transmitted from person to person through touch or breathing too close. We all had to navigate the unknown of a global invisible virus together. What I was going through had to be faced in isolation to protect me from picking up the virus that would only serve to complicate my vulnerable health further.

---

[1] https://www.skagitregionalhealth.org/programs-services/heart-and-vascular/education-and-resources/signs-of-a-stroke

After an eternity of lying on a bed too small for me, with my head on a crinkly coated foam mini pillow and the hustle surrounding me, I was transferred to a room a few floors above. An older, frail man lay on one of the two beds divided by a curtain. A team of three nurse assistants, all masked, gloved, and dressed in scrubs, slid me by holding the edges of a sheet from the gurney onto the bright white sheeted mattress. It was much more comfortable than what was downstairs. I randomly wondered if they had these big, adjustable beds with the TV remote built in for everyone admitted to the hospital, or was it just for those of us they needed to make comfortable to either face a long stay or worse who were in our final days as *"comfort measures."*

After getting tucked in, I was given the rules by the apparent alpha of the two nurses. Wisps of gray framed her freckled, lined, thin face. She was assertive and serious. The woman seemed very rigid and frightening as she dictated those rules to me.

Rule One: Stay in my room with the door closed. It was meant to reduce my risk of catching COVID. The only time it would open would be from the other side when a nurse or doctor would come to see me to check my vital signs, give me medication, or deliver food.

Rule Two: Push the button when I need to use the bathroom. I couldn't walk there unaided, so they referred to me as " *fall risk.*" I never got comfortable with the concept of supervised toileting. But I get it. Nurses do this every day, and to them, body parts and their functions are just part of the job and not a big deal. To someone like me, who is by nature a private person and who likes my alone time in the bathroom, this "fall risk" escort rule was a tough one that took some adjusting.

My room was surprisingly spacious and quiet. A slight warmth of home with my own TV and a shared bathroom with my roommate. It was a welcome relief to the tight quarters and pace of the emergency room. After hours of fear and uncertainty, this space felt safe. It quelled the fact that no one I loved, let alone knew, could be at my bedside, talking to me, making sense of what was happening, or discussing what we should do next. I was on my own and lonely. I closed my eyes in prayer, eventually letting myself sleep with faith and belief I would, in fact, wake up.

Being an African-American middle-aged man with high blood pressure, Type 2 diabetes, and a family history of strokes, I was at a much higher risk of having another stroke compared to most people. This was just the beginning of a long journey. I not only had to fight to recover from the trauma my body had just experienced, but my battle would continue indefinitely to prevent this from happening all over again.

Social workers, therapists, and dieticians evaluated my diet, exercise, stressors, and the environmental factors that may have contributed to landing me in this predicament. My self-care education began. I realized I'd not noticed my own stress as an intangible force with the tentacles of an octopus. Its broad reach and tight squeeze are only shrugged off by creating barriers of self-preservation.

Through prayer, I pledged to God that if I survived this stroke, I would change my ways. No more sugar and fried foods. More exercise and walking. I would embrace daily prayer and friendship to keep me positive and grounded.

> *Dear Lord, stand beside me as I fight to recover and I will live a healthier life. A second chance would be a miracle and the result of your will. Thank you for placing me in the path of the healing hands and hearts caring for me here at White Plains.*

As the days ran together, I lost track of the calendar. Thankfully, Clayton had picked up a bag of clothes, my cell phone, and a charger from home to drop off with the security guards at the hospital. To cut through isolation, my favorite evening nurse would bring me a tablet so I could see and talk with Deana, friends, and family. I would tire easily trying to collect my words and speak enough to be understood. If only for a little while, this helped me feel connected.

After a week in the same room, the guy behind the curtain was going home. Our interactions had been limited. We shared an unspoken mutual respect for privacy and overheard conversations without prying into why we were both there or follow-up questions. The same day he was discharged, I was moved to a smaller private room. With the hospital beyond capacity with COVID cases, my move freed up space for two new patients in the bigger room.

Going from an active life traveling the world in the military, the enormity of living in the Big Apple, and interacting with a large congregation of people, I experienced what a newly convicted felon must feel when confined to a prison cell. In my case, I was not held captive by handcuffs or jail cell bars but trapped by my own body.

James, a fellow usher at the church, checked on me a couple of times a week via a video call he'd arranged through the nurse's station. James assured me he was keeping our congregation updated, and that they were praying for me at Saturday and Sunday services as well as Wednesday night Bible study. It was the support of the people in my life and my faith in God that helped me to get through the despair I felt while in the hospital. It was tough, but I was grateful to be alive.

The last week at White Plains Hospital, a team of therapists came to my room to give me their assessments. Physical therapy will help me walk again unaided. Speech therapy would be employed to help me find my words and elevate my voice so I could be heard. Swallow therapy with the goal of graduating from soft food and liquids back to solids without choking or aspirating into my lungs. This began my road to recovery.

> Nothing is impossible...the word itself says *"I'm possible!"*
>
> ~ *Audrey Hepburn*

Chapter Five

LOOKING FOR MYSELF

fter three weeks at White Plains Hospital, on a Friday evening, I was transported to Burke Rehabilitation Hospital, one of the best rehabilitation hospitals in the tri-state area - less than five miles from my apartment.

They brought me here in an ambulance. I was immediately placed in a hospital room with an older man who was unable to speak and had also experienced a stroke. He was temperamental and combative at times; the hospital echoed quite often with his thrashing and cursing. He was all-out condescending and rude to his daily housekeepers, who are critical to infection prevention in any hospital setting. I wondered if this behavior was his normal temperament. If he used derogatory descriptors for the women in his life by picking out a flaw and swinging it around like a medieval spike ball on a chain, wielding it with the sole intention to inflict pain on those intended to solely take care of him.

Making someone else hurt to quell his own? Maybe it was derived from the frustration of his stroke that he didn't know how to manage. Or perhaps he was too tired and fatigued by looking at the same walls every day. We never found a way to communicate or really find companionship. I don't think anyone else considered him good company, at least in that hospital. I only knew him as Mr. Henderson. It would be only an occasional side glance through the curtain between us that was momentarily pulled back - we were invisible to each other. Over time, by being polite and cooperative with the people crucial to my recovery, I found out that he began to follow my example to calm his temper a bit.

A hospital stay, especially after a stroke, can be an emotionally and physically demanding experience. It's easy to let our emotions run high and lash out at those around us. However, maintaining calmness and politeness towards the hospital staff is not just a matter of courtesy; it also plays a crucial role in your recovery process. I can't further acknowledge that a hospital environment can be overwhelming and stressful. A patient's interactions with hospital staff can either enhance or detract from your emotional well-being. But I'm here to tell you that compassion can make a world of difference. If you interact with the hospital staff calmly and politely, your needs are better understood and concerns well-addressed. It clears a space for open and clear exchange of information, ensuring that your needs are met and optimized if necessary. Stress and anxiety can take a toll on your emotions, but these people are still there to help you with your stress, ensuring that you remain calm and stable, which is essential for healing. They're professionals working long hours under immense pressure, but they're known to dedicate their time appropriately to taking care of every patient. Therefore, they deserved our gratitude and respect, our acknowledgment of their efforts, and our appreciation for their role in our recovery. Whenever I had to deal with them, I preferred approaching them with a calm and polite demeanor.

Not knowing how long I'd be there, I defined myself as a good patient by keenly following the instructions of my doctors and therapists. Every hour felt like it was eating me up; I didn't like this feeling and wanted it gone. My whole body was chained to an excruciating bedrest, with all the machines lined over my head. I wanted to fix what was wrong with me and go home healthy as a stallion galloping through the green hills.

On Friday, I recall the weekend was a little mellow, without a special agenda other than another assessment for occupational, physical, and speech therapy. Other than that, I was able to just rest, watch TV, and acclimate to my new space for most of the day. It was just another day at the facility.

It was the strangest feeling of being trapped inside my own body and mind. I could think, and I could move. But there was a certain disconnection I felt from the life skills I'd picked up as a child. Then suddenly and abruptly, those everyday routines I'd grown into, as simple as brushing my teeth or combing my hair, became scattered like puzzle pieces, not sure until you put it back together if any pieces are missing and lost forever.

I learned that weakness or immobility are very common after-effects of a stroke. In fact, most people are known to experience some type of limitation in muscle movement. Hemiplegia and hemiparesis are the two most common conditions after a stroke, identified by the inability to move muscles voluntarily. Hemiplegia refers to severe paralysis of one side of the body that turns out to be painful, followed by stiffness or spasms in the muscles. In the worst-case scenario, the muscles can even become totally redundant. Whereas Hemiparesis is less severe, characterized by weakness on one side of the body, mostly observable in the extremities, such as the hands. This condition can make it very difficult to perform even the most basic daily tasks; it affects the patient's ability to grasp and release objects. It can also cause loss of balance, difficulty walking, and muscle fatigue.

They weren't allowing any visitors because of Rule One, which applied to all hospitals. I was able to talk often to Deana, my siblings, colleagues, friends, and my cousin who lived in the area. The well-wishes and the power of prayers began circling around me with the beauty of butterflies in a field. The strength of others and their committed support of me lifted and pushed me through to get better despite how difficult it was.

The Burke staff obviously knew what they were doing. Beyond being supportive and helpful, they developed therapy plans focused on me individually. Dr. Andrew Abdou, a board-certified doctor in Physical Medicine and Rehabilitation, led a team that all worked together to set goals and benchmarks as a roadmap to reducing my blood pressure, stabilizing my diabetes, and finding the life skills I'd lost.

They took me to a room that echoed with the rhythmic hum of various exercise machines. I saw the other therapists chanting their words of engagement to their patients, guiding them through their challenging journey.

Upon entering that room, it occurred to me that I was embarking upon the daunting task of rebuilding my life after the mark my stroke had left upon me. With determination etched in my eyes, I ventured through the unfamiliar terrain of the therapy room with the aid of a walker. My therapist stood by my side, offering me both encouragement and technical expertise to regain control over my body. The whole experience was a slow and arduous one as I tried to grapple with each support with the limitations imposed by my weakened muscles. Simple tasks that were once second nature became monumental challenges.

Dr. Abdou became my lifeline, visiting me almost daily. He's specialized in post-stroke neuro-rehabilitation. As a Doctor of Osteopathic Medicine, he focuses on the mind, body, and spirit and acted as my own personal quarterback, calling the plays that would ultimately drive us down the field to the goal line. His knowledge and compassion offered a welcome boost of hope and optimism.

After Monday, these therapies were eventually scheduled every day for an hour. It was how to re-learn to brush my teeth, wash my face, take a shower, and put on my clothes, socks, and shoes. Then, independently sit up, stand, walk down the hallway, and eventually climb the stairs.

With a solid and consistent team of therapists assigned to me at Burke, an Occupational Therapist, Lisa Hawkins, began the long journey of re-teaching me the cognitive and functional skills of everyday life, right down to basic grooming. So many people who have never experienced occupational therapy don't really know what they do. I didn't until the stroke. This helped me to understand exactly how occupational therapy could help me.

Figure 2: *Occupational Therapy Chart for OTPs.*[2]

Elisa-Marie Santobello was my speech therapist. She took a broad-spectrum approach in helping me to find my words, regain my ability to swallow without choking, and improve the way I projected my voice in order to be heard. She always said, *"Al, I want you to be able to say I love you to Deana so she can hear it!"* Our goal was to find better function within whatever my new normal would be. It's the little things that became big for us.

---

[2] https://www.tota.org/assets/FINAL_OT%20ESSA%20Admin_4-25-22.pdf

The physical therapists who helped me would focus on building muscle strength, mobility, balance, and flexibility using a variety of bands, weights, and machines.

The whole process was a symphony of effort, sweat, and triumph. I was bound to engage in a series of exercises designed to strengthen my weakened limbs and improve my balance. The parallel bars became a physical support system, allowing me to rediscover the sensation of putting one foot in front of the other.

The road to recovery was marked by small victories. I still remember the joy on my face radiating through the room the first time I managed to stand unassisted; it inspired both the therapists and fellow patients alike. My doctor, too, celebrated these milestones.

The journey was not without setbacks. There were days when fatigue threatened to overpower my resolve, the weight of which seemed insurmountable. Yet, in those moments, the support of my fellow therapists provided a lifeline of encouragement.

As my cognitive functions improved, my entire care team explained the impacts the stroke had on me physically and mentally in understandable terms. As my brain fog began to clear and fatigue subsided, I began to fully realize how lucky I was to progress back from this. A sense of gratitude and a sense of purpose filled my heart. I knew I wanted to help others and their families who've gone through a similar experience. Deeply rooted in my faith with a desire to serve, as the weeks, months, and now years have gone by since my stroke, I've become a trusted, empathetic resource for fellow veterans, members of our church, friends, and even a wide net of total strangers.

Having lived with high blood pressure (HBP) for years, it's not important to be on an HBP med. It's critical to be prescribed the 'right' HBP medication. And then actually take it as prescribed. Not only to prevent a stroke, but the wrong medication for your unique body chemistry can lead to problems like erratic blood pressure, fatigue, weight gain or loss, dizziness, and debilitating weakness. Not to overlook the potential of a deadly heart disease.

I will admit I didn't have a consistent routine with taking my medications prior to the stroke. The prevention of a catastrophic health event wasn't recognized until the catastrophe actually happened. Only after my stroke, I became more aware of the negative impact of eating the wrong food, such as processed and fried foods and too much salt. I thought I had been living a healthy lifestyle. Overall, I ate well and was mindful of balancing my food intake and exercise. In reality, I was off track in many ways, but I never thought this would be real and would actually happen to me.

While there are typically two kinds of strokes, everyone experiences it differently. Some lose muscle control in their face, have difficulty walking, overall weakness, loss of coordination on one side of the body, trouble swallowing, slurred speech, and lightheadedness. I experienced many of these symptoms. The mission at Burke was to put me on the right path toward fixing the consequences of my stroke. I was blessed to have Dr. Abdou monitoring and managing my road to recovery step by step.

Meditate upon this Psalm of Protection: Psalm: 91, three times a day. We are acknowledging God as being the Great Physician and Ultimate Healer while praying for the restoration and healing of our immediate and extended family members who are experiencing some form of sickness within the body. Thank you and God Bless you!

Chapter Six

GOING HOME

T he first time I saw Deana in months was the day I was discharged from Burke. She had been in Indianapolis with her mother and then when she arrived in New York she was staying at our Mamaroneck apartment. She was cleaning, organizing, and getting it ready for my homecoming. She had been working remotely while in Indianapolis and taking care of a few work commitments but then organized herself to come to New York to transition me home.

Deana didn't tell me that her mom had died a month earlier due to COVID complications until after she got me out of Burke and I was settled at home in the apartment. All along, she'd been helping to coordinate my care and lifting my spirits with her positive energy while she not only navigated her mom's health crisis but saw her through her final days and laid her to rest without me at her side. There's a weight I'll never shake knowing that I wasn't with her through her saddest moments.

This taught me that through the good and bad times in my life, I always want to be present for my loved ones. Staying healthy not only for me but also for Deana became another boost of motivation.

My heart filled with love and gratitude to finally see my wife in person after all of this time being isolated with strangers – people I'd never be able to repay for their care and kindness.

I was strong enough to be released without using any devices like a cane, walker, or wheelchair, but I continued to have difficulty with my balance. Still unsteady, Deana had worked with our apartment maintenance team to install a toilet, shower head with cord, and bath security rails. Before leaving Burke, Lisa guided us through ordering a shower bench, bedside commode, raised toilet seat, and a side railing to help me get in and out of bed.

The first few weeks at home, home healthcare would come to my apartment. I had all of the resources in line and tailored to my specific needs to continue my path back to finding a renewed, stronger, and healthier Al Smith.

My rehab felt slow, but by the time it ended, I had built some muscle and stood steadier. After many doctors' appointments, outpatient rehab, and coordinating with Dr. Susan Soeiro, Deana and I went to meet with my new neurological specialist at her clinic, a few miles from our apartment.

A bright, beautiful Asian woman, Dr. Amy Hua is a neurologist focused on muscle and peripheral nerve disease. She was a smart soul, with the bedside manner of an angel, and young enough to be my daughter. She spent time getting to know me. In fact, both of us asked questions, explored our lifestyles, and analyzed the unique complexities of my particular situation. She sat beside me and never stood above me. Her fascination with medicine was apparent, as was her passion for the puzzle of chronic disease management.

Though it was my left side that was impaired, Dr. Hua explained that I had a right basal ganglia ischemic stroke. This impacts the part of the brain that controls language, movement, moods, emotions, motor learning, and intuition. I also had hypophonia, making my speech soft, a personality trait unrecognized amongst the old Al Smith. I could speak and understand when spoken to, but struggled with finding, coordinating, and projecting my words. Swallowing was also different and more challenging. I had to learn to focus on eating slowly and thoroughly chewing my food.

Three Types of Stroke

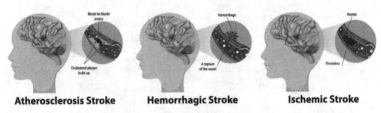

Atherosclerosis Stroke   Hemorrhagic Stroke   Ischemic Stroke

Figure 3: Types of Strokes[3]

With a team of outpatient therapists, their goals centered around building my overall strength by giving me in-bed exercises, walking with me within the apartment or down the hallways, and eventually stair-climbing the interior apartment stairwell. I relied on Deana or a physical therapist to do daily standing and sitting exercises.

The speech therapist helped me with my voice level and cadence. Additionally, she helped me with regaining reasoning and decision-making by giving me books, logic exercises, calculating money, creating and keeping a schedule, assisting me in focusing on taking my time with word problems, and any cognitive and therapeutic programming you can imagine. I'd master one challenge, and there'd be another in their toolkit.

My occupational therapist helped by building coordination on my left side. The therapy consisted of specifically picking up and holding things in my left hand, strengthening my grip, and pulling and stretching my arm and shoulder. I worked with dough, rolling pins, spreading my fingers out, and rolling a towel out and forward, and reaching my hand and arm up along the wall to strengthen it.

We changed my diet because my blood pressure was still elevated and difficult to control. With a nurse assigned to us from

---

[3] https://www.linkedin.com/pulse/recognizing-gendered-signs-impending/

my employer's health insurance, she'd call to speak with Deana and me about my progress, nutrition, and diet and helped us navigate through the insurance process.

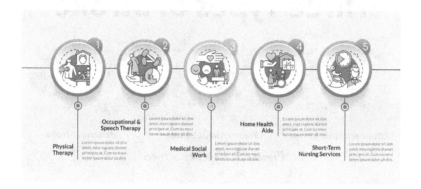

As an Army Veteran, after 16 years of service, including my time in Iraq, there were resources through the Veteran's Administration (VA) where my primary care physician practiced. I was able to get supplies like bed liners, Diabetes screening tools and a blood pressure cuff. I was given nutrition information, and a nurse monitored the blood pressure and blood sugar readings that Deana added to the patient portal every week.

My exercise regimen consisted of going to Burke Rehabilitation Fitness Center to work out and perform the exercises that the athletic training staff created for me. I continued to improve upon my fitness goals of strength building, core, flexibility, and balance exercises. My target was two to three times a week at Burke Fitness Center and the gym in my apartment building in between. Deana and I would walk around the neighborhood, go to the grocery store, wander around Harbor Island, and birdwatch.

Sometimes, on the weekends, Deana and I would cook together. Deana was usually the sous chef, and I'm the culinary master with a true enjoyment in its creativity. We'd find new ways to prepare brussels sprouts, kale, collard greens, cabbage, salmon, soups, chili, and other vegetarian meals.

We'd relax in the evenings after dinner, watching sports or binging the latest streaming series. We'd snuggle on the couch to call or Zoom friends. Life was regaining some sense of normalcy. I'd lost about 40 pounds and was on track to fully recover.

I was proud of my progress until the end of August when lethargy came over me. My left leg and foot began to drag when I walked, and I was struggling to urinate. I laid low, but right before Labor Day, I had a fall in the apartment and reinjured and bruised my left shoulder, arm, and knee. The area was still sore from my stroke fall but had been healing. I was weak again and in pain. With a persistent low-grade fever and far too many hours of sleep, my primary care physician suspected a urinary tract infection. I couldn't stand or get to the car, so Deana called 911.

Chapter Seven

DÉJÀ VU

H ere we go again... Déjà vu moment; the paramedics returned to the same apartment they had visited months earlier to, once again, to carry me down the stairs into the ambulance waiting to escort me back to White Plains Hospital. I was immediately diagnosed with a severe urinary tract infection and sepsis. I began incurring more falls with weakness, swelling in my legs, and pain in the left ankle.

The doctors resorted to a blood transfusion that eventually improved my condition overnight; I was finally able to sleep. After an eight-day stay which consisted of celebrating my birthday virtually with family and close monitoring by hospital staff, the in-patient physical therapy team helped me to gain enough strength to be discharged with a walker and transported me via an ambulance to the United Hebrew Inpatient Rehabilitation Hospital, a sub-acute rehabilitation hospital.

As soon as I was under the close watch of sub-acute rehabilitation staff, I was back to daily occupational and physical therapy to rebuild my strength and balance. Over the month while I was there, I had to re-re-learn how to walk, lift myself, and stand with better balance. To avoid falls, I had to summon help every time I wanted to get out of bed, go to the bathroom, or to my bedside chair. I also needed help with my grooming and bathing.

This setback was disheartening. It chipped away at my spirits at a time when I thought I was able to see beyond the stroke. I truly thought I was on the brink of regaining my active lifestyle. I'd slipped back into a sense of loneliness with the cellular and internet service patchy in the century-old brick building, finding it difficult to communicate with my wife, family, and friends. To add to my isolation, COVID outbreaks were still on the rise, so I had to stay in my room most of the time with limited human contact. Depressing.

A few days prior to my projected discharge, I began to feel weaker, lethargic, and not myself again. My blood pressure was elevated and erratic. Tests revealed that I had another urinary tract infection. Starting over with a new antibiotic, it took several days for me to clear the infection and finally begin to feel better. At that point, I could continue with the therapy. My strength kept returning each day.

With demanding work and unrelenting effort, I was slowly able to regain my strength. I was able to walk, but this time with a customized foot brace on my left ankle and foot. They diagnosed me with Drop Foot Syndrome, which forced me to learn how to walk with this makeshift lightweight plastic brace and ace bandage until my permanent Ankle Foot Orthosis (AFO) was designed for me.

Well enough to be discharged, I was excited that I was finally able to go home. Deana was able to visit with me and my therapists to learn how to properly tend to the foot ankle brace and ace bandage.

Once the AFO came in, I found it difficult at first to learn to walk with the device without it being too tight on my foot and ankle. At times, it hurt my knee when I'd walk around. I learned to wear it for longer periods of time and got used to it. I found out that I eventually walked better with it.

I have to say, Deana went so far beyond her vows of "*in sickness and health.*" She worked with a local private care provider to have an in-home health aide come into the apartment several days during

41

the week to help me with my daily care regimen. I didn't have to use a cane, walker, or wheelchair, but I needed help with my balance and support walking without falling. Our in-home healthcare aide helped me in and out of bed, coached my exercises, and helped me get around the apartment. She also prepared meals, helped with the laundry and light housework, and stayed home with me while Deana worked remotely or ran errands.

Due to a shortage of speech therapists, I was only able to receive physical and occupational therapy again. However, between our in-home health aide and the other therapists, I gradually got stronger and had faith in a better outlook and prognosis. We were able to go back to the apartment gym to train.

Over time, I started to see that I could move my foot, toes, and ankle. The progress was tangible, which motivated me even more. When I was at United Hebrew, I was unable to put weight on my left foot and ankle or walk steadily.

I was pleased with this progress and knew it'd take more time and work to recover fully.

When the insurance company determined, they were finished covering my therapies, we were blessed to meet Gina Basalo, a personal trainer. I believe God had a hand in putting her in our path at precisely the moment we needed her. Deana had popped into one of her favorite New Rochelle consignment shops to treasure hunt. She chatted with the shop owner, Marie, who had become a friend and was asking Deana how I was doing. Expressing concern that I still needed support building mobility, balance, and strength, she enthusiastically recommended Gina and her years of experience as a personal trainer.

On Tuesdays and Thursdays, Deana and I would drive to Gina's home in the Bronx, where she'd train both of us in her training studio. As her first stroke patient, she'd sought the guidance of a physical therapist she knew to ensure my safety. Exercises were tailored specifically to our individual capabilities and designed for each of us to reach our desired goals. When we started with Gina,

I wasn't able to lift my left arm high enough for my stance to be parallel to the floor. The connection between my arm and brain wasn't working. They weren't talking. Gina figured out how we could work on my muscle memory. After training together for ten weeks, I could raise my arm over my head.

At 4'11", she is a powerhouse and wasn't intimidated by my size. She's the kind of person that, when working with a client, you are the center of her focus - not easily distracted. It was fun and bonding. She gave us skills we could do at home with small weights, floor core exercises, strength training bands, and virtual classes.

In addition to working with Gina, Deana and I began working out one on one with a Pilates instructor once a week for several months. This training helped with my flexibility and mobility recovery as well.

No doubt! By taking certain vitamins and practicing certain habits, you can improve your health and immune system. A more detailed summary of the vitamins and processes is below:

Echinacea
Immune-boosting Echinacea is well-known for supporting the immune system and may reduce cold severity and duration. Consider taking Echinacea tablets or sipping tea. It is often advised during cold and flu season.

Elderberry
Elderberry has antioxidants and antiviral properties. Flu symptoms might be reduced in duration and severity. Elderberry supplements and syrup are used during flu season. Follow the dosing instructions.

B12
Vitamin B12 is needed to make red blood cells and maintain a healthy nervous system. Maintains vitality and well-being. Vitamin B12 supplements should be used if you're deficient, which is common in some diets.

Alvis E. Smith

Vitamin D
Vitamin D supports bone health and the immunological system. Preventing respiratory infections may suffice. If your sun exposure is limited, you may want to take vitamin D supplements, eat vitamin D-rich foods, or get some sun.

Vitamin C
Vitamin C is an antioxidant that aids iron absorption and immunological function. Thus, it reduces cold intensity and length. Vitamin C-rich foods include citrus fruits and berries, or you can take supplements.

Multivitamin
Multivitamins provide a wide spectrum of essential nutrients, improving your health and filling nutritional gaps. Choose a high-quality, customized multivitamin and take it as directed.

Zinc
Zinc helps the immune system, wound healing, and DNA creation. It may reduce respiratory infections' severity and duration. Take zinc supplements or eat zinc-rich foods. Do not exceed recommended doses.

Warm liquids
Warm drinks like herbal teas or broths can relieve pain, hydrate, and soothe the throat while sick. Drinking warm liquids should be a frequent habit, especially when sick.

Gargle with Listerine
Gargling with Listerine reduces throat pathogens. Listerine should be part of your oral hygiene routine, especially while you're unwell.

These activities can improve health, but they cannot substitute a good diet, sleep, regular exercise, and proper hygiene. Consult a doctor before adding new substances. If you're taking medication or managing a health issue, this is crucial. God bless and protect you!

Chapter Eight

⌁

2500 MILES

T he wake of an unexpected health crisis has more than medical and physical consequences. It throws your priorities in the air like confetti. Adapting to a disability can be difficult. We take our health for granted until it's gone. It's easy to worry about what we leave behind. Even if you cannot change your handicap or wish it away, you can change how you think about and deal with it. Although you're in charge of your life, there are many ways to boost your independence, empowerment, and perspective.

The bulk of us expect long, healthy lives. Thus, a disabling disease or injury might cause many uncomfortable feelings and fears. You may be wondering how to find love, a job, or happiness again. Living with a disability is difficult, but it doesn't have to be tragic.

Before the stroke, I planned my days around others to cover the to-do list and accomplish as much as possible. I had been spending so much time driving through the greater New York City area in an attempt to get everything done, but the job was never done. It just kept coming and juggling with many things became very difficult. And with COVID, it was even harder.

Deana and I owned a rental condo near my apartment. It was a great investment with income that was more than enough to cover my Mamaroneck apartment rent. While the COVID vaccination was undergoing development in 2022, the housing market began to boom again.

The COVID pandemic wrecked the housing market. This volatility was driven by interest rate swings, demand and supply changes, and other factors. Property prices skyrocketed due to great demand and low supply.

At the start of the epidemic, the US economy went into recession, lowering mortgage rates. This, together with the desire for real estate to accommodate telecommuters, quickly raised housing demand. However, inventory was limited. Development was slow when it happened. The hefty prices made buying a home during the pandemic impossible. During this time, many buyers left the property market to wait for stability. Real Estate developers and banks raised mortgage rates, resulting in many overpriced sales.

However, as soon as the world started getting back on its feet again, mortgage rates began to fall again as more buyers entered the market. These were promising signs because property prices had stayed steady, increasing buyers. Buyers had to present themselves prepared with pre-approved financing to make an offer over the asking price. Many properties were receiving multiple offers within hours of being listed. And, honestly, I couldn't fathom being a landlord any longer.

It appeared the stars were beginning to align for us. With our tenants' lease contract nearing expiration, and after their departure, many months of renovation, we decided to list our condominium we owned located between White Plains and Scarsdale. It was sold within ten weeks.

Days, months, and even years after my stroke, I couldn't really plan ahead and anticipate what tomorrow would have for me. I abruptly became focused on finding my strength and former self, and that gradually became an imposed priority. It seemed that my body consistently betrayed my mind, resulting in a negotiation between the two.

The life Deana and I planned together was in jeopardy. I was not prepared to risk her career. In New York, she worked at home as per practice through the peak of COVID, which happened to coincide with the early days of my stroke recovery. She already had to give up a promotion opportunity because she couldn't be back on campus in Arizona.

As I improved and the pandemic restrictions relaxed, Deana and I decided to let go of the New York apartment and made our move back to Tempe. It was only a matter of time before she would be back in her ASU athletics office, working face-to-face with her team and the student-athletes they served. We couldn't allow my stroke recovery to compromise her career.

With the decision made, we began planning the transition of my care and our move cross-country. Two years and three months after the stroke, a new chapter unfolded at the beginning of July 2022. This would involve a whole new team of doctors and therapists. An ASU doctor colleague of Deana's navigated us to the Mayo Clinic in Tempe. They made it so easy, proactively setting me up with a complete care team that we'd meet within days after our arrival in Tempe. They adopted me from day one.

Once the movers loaded the truck, we had six days to drive from our home in White Plains, NY, to the home Deana and I had rented in early 2015 in Tempe. We sat down together and methodically planned our trip, including two days of visiting Deana's family in Indianapolis and finally hosting a proper celebration of life to honor her mother, who passed away from COVID early in the pandemic in April 2020.

With our dark blue Acura SUV, loaded with our treasures not suitable for a moving vehicle, we headed out on our long journey within an hour after the movers left.

The embrace of Deana's siblings and the opportunity to be together to honor her mom was cathartic. We'd gather around the table at Deana's brother's home, with the warmth of delicious meals, prayed, shared stories, laughed, and enjoyed our time together with a greater depth of meaning and purpose.

I sat by her family and felt the warmth in the small dwelling we dined in, thinking about how grateful I was for this time with my extended family. The subtle hum of laughter and the distant echo of debates created a symphony that reiterated why these moments were so vital.

In the midst of all the rush and bustle of attending doctors' appointments and physical therapy, it's easy to become caught up in these tasks, deadlines, and the outside world's constant pace. Whenever I was in Indianapolis with my loved ones, time seemed to slow down, allowing us to make memories that will last forever. I learned that these little moments have tremendous importance. Lively talks, tranquil evenings spent fooling around with others, and shared dinners when we told stories and passed around dishes - all wove a fabric of love and connection.

The smiles of my wife and the comforting presence of my in-laws harbored a feeling of thankfulness within me. We shared joy when we ate a well-prepared meal. We sat in silence while we watched the sunset and shared excitement when we conveyed our plans.

During these times, the outside world melts away, leaving love and understanding. Instead of annoyance, family members' quirks are amusing. Learning and professional progress can come from distinctions. It was during these moments I learned that accepting each other's unique personalities takes time and strength.

I'm very grateful for these few moments of relief when we'd assemble for a holiday feast. I appreciate small moments like these. We're grateful for the laughter that fills the house, the bonds that strengthen each day, and the serendipity that led us here.

This vacation was more than a break from routine; it reminded us of what matters. My heart was full of precious memories. These memories contain our love, laughter, and shared experiences. The simple act of being together gave me many reasons to be glad. I enjoyed the warmth of my family, the most important gift, while the fire burned and night fell.

While the pandemic had a horrible and tragic impact on our world in so many ways, for some of us, it instilled a deeper sense of gratitude for the simple moments in life. With the isolation of COVID and the stroke, I have a newfound appreciation for an authentic smile, the time I spend with those I care about, and genuinely listening to what's important to them.

Now, I realize how precarious life is, and every shared moment is more important than before. I discovered solace and healing in Deana's family. Their unwavering support at moments of weakness and acceptance soothed my spirit. I now think about things like how a loved one's smile can heal wounds and lift spirits, nothing minor matters.

The stroke, which caused unexpected complications, reminded us of life's transience. It changed my priorities, making me appreciate every minute and value the people who make life worth living. Above that, the pandemic's isolation reinforced this insight, emphasizing the importance of human connection in the hassle of life. I found beauty in the ordinary and joy in the routine now that I'm surrounded by family. Eating together can become a feast of thanks, and a simple chat can become a standalone experience. Unfortunately, this melody of existence was formerly taken for granted.

Hearing, especially actual hearing, is an art. Remember that every family member's word matters and every story shows a unique perspective. As I listen, I realize that our tales are intertwined and that our experiences are connected with laughter, tears, and silent understanding.

This difficult and persistent phase of my life has shown me the tremendous beauty that sprang from adversity. This encounter showed me the value of authentic interactions. Adversity showed me the masterpiece of love and togetherness in my heart.

Thus, in the glow of these moments we had, I am appreciating both what was and what is. This is a rediscovery and celebration of smiles, stories, and warmth from being together that are no longer transitory moments; they have become anchors in the ever-changing sea of life, helping me stay rooted in the present.

After a long, tearful goodbye, we drove from Indianapolis to St. Louis, Missouri, to see my cousin and Deana's aunt, whom we hadn't seen in two years. Though it was a brief one-night stay, we talked for hours and enjoyed a wonderful visit together.

With challenges sitting idle for long periods of time, we took advantage of the six days we had before having to meet the movers on the other end. I drove in the mornings and Deana in the afternoon, when I'd experience an onset of fatigue. We'd pass the time listening to podcasts and gospel and jazz music, reading and napping. With additional overnight stops in Oklahoma City, Oklahoma, and Albuquerque, New Mexico; our final six and a half hours to our home in warm and balmy Tempe, Arizona, was easy with the joy of knowing we'd be home in our own bed and together, without geography or COVID separating us.

Though tired from travel, my heart jumped when we entered our Tempe neighborhood. Familiar, large stucco homes framed by manicured rock gardens topped with terracotta tiles. Our two-story cream stucco home, with brown brick accents and surrounded by established oversized succulents and cacti, rested in the quiet and privacy of a cul-de-sac and backed up to a large lake.

I'd forgotten how much different the desert air was compared to anywhere else in the country. Hot, dry heat, with a subtle sweet, earthy aroma of patchouli laced with the citrus of our neighbor's lemon tree. Filled with a sense of peace, my heart lightened with a belief I was right where I was supposed to be – away from the chaos of New York City life and immersed in the warmth and security of home with Deana.

Chapter Nine

LESSONS LEARNED

Y ou don't know what you don't know - This is why experiences –
good and bad – make us grow into who we become throughout
our lifetime. We never stop evolving and learning. You go
through life hearing about other people's injuries, ailments, and
illnesses but never realize the depth of their experience until it
happens to you.

Sympathy and agreement are easy to sense and nod to from
afar. Life forces us to confront the complexities of another's journey,
which develops genuine empathy. Our shared experiences allow us
to practice empathy, which brings out the strength and fragility of
which we were unaware.

This seems evident in health problems. We hear stories of people
who overcame illnesses and injuries, but unless we manage our own
health issues, these tales won't be fully obvious. Anecdotes from
others become live blueprints for uncharted territories.

We may piece together our humanity via our varied experiences,
from the delight of being healthy to the difficulties of being sick.
We often overlook our bodies' sophisticated mechanics and flawless
systems while we're healthy. Only when the music falters do we
realize our fragility and pliability. Knowing that one's well-being

is a delicate dance between an endless number of variables can change how we view our own and others' experiences. The person formerly defined by their ailment shows the fortitude, perseverance, and tenacity of the human spirit. Scars, once considered fighting wounds, now symbolize survival and recovery.

As we navigate life, we are reminded that experience is the greatest equalizer. It connects the familiar and unknown by turning pity into empathy and building a shared understanding beyond individual stories. Every attempt and achievement becomes a stroke on our collective narrative, illustrating the underlying interconnection of the human experience. Thus, we grow, learn, and broaden our perspectives, accepting the patchwork of occurrences that shape us into the marvelously diverse people we are meant to be.

Having a stroke imposed an education on the complexities and connections between physical, mental, and spiritual wellness that I had no idea I'd ever receive.

- I took the diverse medical resources and services for granted.
- The value of having an advocate when you can't be one for yourself. Deana stepped into that role fluidly, without hesitation, before I was even able to ask her for help. Strokes can make communication difficult or impossible. In situations like these, the work of a support system is especially important since they are responsible for ensuring that our rights, preferences, and requirements are stated and respected. They speak up for our best interests, whether it's about our healthcare, choosing a treatment, or meeting daily living needs. Deana helped me connect to my recovery route during vulnerability and adjustment whilst providing me with practical and emotional help.
- I learned that as a stroke survivor, we need a good group of trusted friends and family that we can rely on as backup in times of need.

- A committed internal medicine doctor who can connect us with all the specialists necessary for our comprehensive care is critical.
- A neurologist, a cardiologist, an ophthalmologist, and possibly a urologist are just a few doctors who may be in your circle if you've experienced a stroke. The right team of providers promotes a successful recovery.
- Let's not overlook the value of your team of therapists specializing in speech, occupational, and physical therapy. An advocate to help you with your medication could include a pharmacist.
- I would be completely remiss to not mention how the strength of my church congregation who share a mutual faith in God can lead to recovery. It's not that I expect the sprinkle of holy water on my head to magically reverse time and make the impacts of the stroke disappear. The resiliency in my shared faith in God also helped me to recover. The unwavering support, prayers, and community spirit give my rehabilitation path continued hope and tenacity. The shared belief in a higher power gives me meaning and motivates me to overcome obstacles. The spiritual comfort soothes not only the physical wounds but also the emotional and mental toll of the stroke. I'm reminded that healing is a team effort inspired by faith. Shared reflections and genuine concern from the people around me inspired and strengthened me.

A harsh reality of being human is being imperfect. We are challenged with physical, mental, emotional, and spiritual strife. Some days, we question all of it. With unwavering faith in God comes the belief in the power of our own strength and ability to persevere through adversity.

It's about celebrating the little victories and not letting the setbacks have power over your positivity. Celebrating small victories allows us to recognize and appreciate them—physical, emotional, or circumstantial. They can motivate and inspire when faced with hardship. Although these victories seem small, they represent substantial progress in overcoming problems. Every little improvement in physical mobility, mental clarity, or daily goal completion contributes to total progress. It acknowledges that progress can be made even in difficult situations. This perspective promotes gratitude and prevents difficulties from dictating one's course. It is about changing your mentality to see hurdles as stepping stones rather than stumbling blocks and utilizing positivity to turn challenges into opportunities for personal growth and resilience.

> With men this is impossible, but with God all things are possible.
>
> *- Matthew 19:26 New King James Version*

I learned early on not to let my ego or pride become a barrier to what's right for my recovery. It was emotionally and mentally challenging to not be able to take care of the basics for myself. I discovered great power in seeking help after accepting the vulnerability of healing. Accepting help was a sign of persistence and a turning point. I realized that true strength is the ability to be self-sufficient and know when help is needed. This mindset change allowed me to rely on medical professionals, my friends and family, and my community's support. When I let go of the need to look untouched by bad feelings, I was able to access a network of care that helped me recover. Regaining my independence taught me that asking for help is not a sign of weakness but a step toward healing and growth. I realized this after experiencing humility.

By nature, I'm a reserved and modest person, and I had to let go of that with the people caring for me. Being bathed by a nursing assistant or having someone supervise me while trying to shower myself was foreign and awkward.

Looking back, I notice that I eventually surrendered to my modesty for my own safety and care. Falling in the shower during my weakest moment could have resulted in permanent consequences. My caregivers knew this, and now, I realize they were there not to take control of my vulnerability but to protect it with a depth of human-to-human compassion I'd never known before.

At age 60, I never thought I had to rely on a cane. Little did I know that the cane helped with more than balance. It helped my hands and ability to grip. I became accustomed to challenging the strength and coordination in my left arm and hand to eventually be able to pick things up.

A good recovery plan consists of therapy after being discharged from the hospital. Therapeutic interventions help patients adapt from the hospital to regular life, which can be difficult. Physical therapy, a crucial part, rebuilds strength, mobility, and coordination. Reintegrating basic daily activities is easier with occupational therapy, which builds independence. Speech therapy tackles cognitive and communication issues if needed. Besides physical help, psychological support is crucial. Counseling and mental health treatment helps people cope with anxiety, depression, and other mental health issues that may arise during the healing process. Periodic medical follow-ups and recovery plan changes keep it dynamic and responsive to the individual's changing needs. After hospitalization, a comprehensive rehabilitation plan guides the patient toward a fulfilling and functioning life.

As for myself, I went to Burke, the inpatient rehab facility, for a month to receive daily inpatient therapy for speech, occupational, and physical therapy. All the other responsibilities in my life had been parked. My only job at that point was to focus on my physical recovery and keep my mind strong. I relearned to walk, brush my teeth, comb my hair, and wash my face. As basic and simple as it sounds, it is vital to recovery. Also, sleep is as critical as hydration.

I realized I could either give up and stay at my lowest point forever or keep fighting my way up. Regardless of your location or activity, time passes quickly. Personally, I wasn't ready to lose everything. I realized "I had a choice, a pivotal moment where the direction of my life rested in my hands," like lightning. A choice existed. I learned resilience by facing tremendous challenges. The task was to acknowledge the challenges and decide not to let them define my future. Giving up seemed like accepting someone else's destiny. I actively participated in my recovery rather than avoiding it. I choose to write about overcoming despair and persevering through enormous difficulties. The key was to use the misery to inspire change. I entered the struggle knowing that it would be difficult, but I understood that every step forward was a win, reclaiming land that had been lost to the shadows. My life, relationships, and goals were too important to give up. In that critical moment, I chose hope over despair, resilience over resignation, and the unshakable will to rise from misery to the spotlight.

Being mindful of your body and the impact of a stroke is key to recovery and regaining a healthy life. Be careful not to ignore how your body feels. You're the only one living in your skin and know it better than anyone.

For the first time in my adult life, I learned to take all my medications correctly without missing a dose, with proper hydration, and at the right times so they'd work effectively.

I was required to establish and keep a low-sugar, high-fiber, healthy diet with fruits, vegetables, and protein. Physical exercise is also important. Whole-body stretching and physical exercise three to four times a week will fight off illness and help prevent chronic or life-threatening diseases.

Stretching on your wounded side is important to promote flexibility. Pick one new habit at a time, focus on it, and master it. Then, pick another. One methodical and sustainable step at a time. If you live alone like I did, it's important to make connections with others to look out for and check in on each other. Everyone needs someone watching their back.

Your advocates can be your spouse, good friend, or neighbor. If you're a veteran, a nurse case manager can help assess and facilitate your care needs. Some of the important points to consider:

- Maintaining a working phone and having an advocate is critical to staying connected.
- You want to make sure that they know where you live.
- How to access your home, and that they know who's your primary care doctor.
- They should have someone at your workplace to call if they need to reach your employer.
- You want someone close to understand your medications and stay on top of them.
- You and your advocate need to understand your insurance plan, short-term and long-term disability benefits, and if there's Social Security Disability coverage. You want to make sure that you have a good plan and understand how to maximize the benefits.
- Most importantly, make sure your advocate knows your wishes so they can make decisions on your behalf if necessary.

With federal health information protections in place, it's important to be proactive with making your wishes known while you're still healthy. It's a matter of addressing the "What ifs" before they happen. This is where a Living Will document comes into play. You can literally download a template from the internet. It will eliminate confusion, questions, and contention within your family.

A Living Will is a written health care directive that consists of your wishes related to resuscitation, life support, power of attorney designation, and who within your circle of doctors can share medical updates. The Living Will can also include your preferences toward burial, interment, and cremation. I know it's morbid to talk about, but it keeps control of your choices over your care even if you're unable to express your desires at the time.

Trust in the Lord with all your heart,
And lean not on your own understanding;
In all your ways acknowledge Him,
And He shall direct your paths.

- Proverbs 3:5-6 New King James Version

Chapter Ten

∞

MY ARIZONA LIFE

I am not the same Al Smith I was before the stroke. In many ways, I'm better. My journey, comprised of endless doctor appointments, surgeries, physical therapies, and hospital check-ins, made me more mindful of my well-being and self-care. I seemingly became an expert on healthcare. The connections between diet, exercise, and calories consumed versus burned, I was more aware of my body's mechanism than a layman.

The benefits of proper nutrition and exercise for our well-being must be acknowledged. Considering that diet and fitness are more about inside health than external beauty, it's important to recognize their overall benefits. Focusing on internal health includes aesthetics and many things that affect longevity and quality of life. Our fitness is crucial to cardiovascular health, so it's not only for looks. Physical exercise raises the heart rate, which increases blood flow to supply oxygen and nutrients to the cardiovascular system's organs and tissues. This prevents blood clots and blockages in arteries and optimizes organ function.

Gradually, regular age-appropriate exercise becomes more important as we age. To maintain flexibility, strength, and cardiovascular health throughout age, one must tailor physical activity to the body's changing needs. Remember, the goal is to prevent present health concerns and invest in long-term vitality.

Taking in the appropriate nutrition provides the body with the building blocks needed for cell repair, energy production, and immune system function. Vitamin-rich, mineral-rich diets help the body battle oxidative stress and inflammation. Food like this helps prevent chronic diseases.

A healthy diet and regular exercise can usually improve internal health. My healing journey taught me that nutrition and exercise choices affect our health today and in the future. Prioritizing our internal well-being enhances our physical function, which, in turn, goes beyond physical wellness.

Slowly, I continued to regain strength and coordination on my left side. My body chemistry is different. More sensitive. This means that my body is more reactive to variables, medicines, and environmental changes. Blood chemistry involves hormones, nutrients, electrolytes, and other compounds. These levels can vary due to your heritage and genetics, your lifestyle, nutrition intake, and personal healthcare.

After I ended up in the emergency room this summer, I learned that staying hydrated in the Arizona heat should be a top priority for me. Arizona is known for its desert climate with high temperatures and low humidity. Due to the state's varied topography, summers are hot, but weather can vary. Locals and tourists often struggle with temperatures that grow even higher. In addition, the clear sky and plenty of sunshine in Arizona intensify the summer heat. Because there is little cloud cover, the sun's rays beat down on the ground, causing prolonged heat exposure. With the dryness of the air, I hadn't realized the value of keeping a water bottle by my side during gym workouts. I give off sweat profusely when I'm working hard and lose a little too much without replenishing. Lightheaded and dizzy, I staggered and slid down the wall at the gym after working out. With my history, we weren't risking the potential of another stroke, so I was taken to the Dignity Health emergency room for an evaluation.

I'll never forget the look on Deana's face when she arrived at the hospital. Fear and determination narrowed her chocolate eyes and puckered her full, heart-shaped lips. The worry I saw quickly drained, replaced by relief and the rise of her broad, beautiful smile. Our eyes met when she peeked through the curtain. I was sitting upright on the gurney, talking to the certified nursing assistant, who was taking my blood pressure.

Deana had been interrupted during a meeting in her office to be told I was enroute to the hospital. She didn't know much more than I'd collapsed, and I was still alive. So many questions and fears ran through her mind as she drove 12 miles to Dignity Health Arizona General Hospital from ASU quietly and in her own head.

With IV fluids onboard, my pre-workout strength and energy were restored. Hours later, late in the afternoon, I was released to Deana. We went home and cooked salmon and veggies. Eating at the coffee table, we binge-watched our favorite series, *Justified*, for the third time.

Seeing Deana after a long time was a powerful and emotional event. I felt anxious, worried, and vulnerable during that time. During this period, loved ones who may have been waiting for updates can console and reassure the individual.

My initial sight of Deana's worried-to-relieving attributes left a lasting impression when she arrived at Burke Rehabilitation Hospital back in April 2020. I was excited to learn that the reunion would be more than just a physical reunion. That first hug was a lovely collision of vulnerability and strength. The tenderness of our embrace transmitted a lot of information without words. The tears released pent-up emotions like fear from uncertainty, relief at the successful surgery, and overwhelming gratitude for her continual support. Our eyes conveyed deep understanding, and our laughter showed our calmness after the storm.

There was and still is work to be done. But I genuinely believe my stroke ultimately saved my life. I survived, which means I've been given the chance to take control of my health. I get to start over – a second round. Not a gift everyone is given. I'm eternally grateful to the people who saved my life, helped me regain what I'd lost, and to the almighty force above that nourished my faith and abated my fear.

I didn't realize it at the time, but Deana also saved my life. Even though she couldn't be with me during those early critical days after the stroke, it was her loving, generous spirit that carried me. She never gave up on me or lost her belief in my recovery. Not everyone can understand what an honor it is to be partnered with a person like her. She's strong, warm, and positive with everyone she meets - and I get to be married to her. I'm honestly not sure how I could have survived and thrived without her.

My diet, sleep patterns, and exercise are all more highly valued to me than ever before. I never miss my Mayo Clinic and VA doctor follow-up appointments, and I've developed my own system, intuitive to me, for managing medications. I've never missed my dosage and regularly ensured my intake.

The 'new' and 'improved' Al Smith actually enjoys drinking a healthy antioxidant fruit smoothie for breakfast, which is hilarious because I'd never pegged myself as a smoothie kind of guy. I look forward to every Tuesday morning and my gym ritual with the guidance of a personal trainer. Most of all, I love Deana's and my evening walks around our neighborhood lake as the Tempe sun is setting. Deana and I hold hands, laugh, and share the day's events.

With COVID restrictions lifted, and my mobility improved, Deana and I decided to jump back into our love of travel with a trip to Seattle, Washington to see my cousin, Alma Jean Cochran.

Back in July 2022, Deana detailed to me her carefully planned vacation, a celebration of life and healing, and the gathering was exciting. I left clinical settings. The promise of the impending adventure gave hope and showed love's persistence in tragedy.

The hospital room, which had been a refuge for a brief time, transformed when it was time to leave. With my wife's help, the wheelchair became a chariot that gave me more freedom. It was a celebration of overcoming the unexpected.

As one of the senior associate athletic directors in Sun Devil Athletics, Deana had a PAC-12 swimming and diving meet in Seattle, and I tagged along so the three of us could enjoy dinner and catch up. Exploring Seattle with Alma Jean and finding new restaurants was a welcoming relief from post-COVID and post-stroke isolation. Just getting on a plane made me feel normal again. I had plans to travel back to Georgia and Alabama in the upcoming year to see family and provide them with proof of life after being apart for years.

Licensed in New York and Georgia, I'm pursuing my Arizona real estate license. Maintaining the concentration to study and retain what I learn has been more challenging than it was years ago. But, with reading, my cognitive skills and focus are improving week by week. The legal and contractual nuances are so different, and the real estate exam is much longer, at about 5.5 hours. So, being able to focus without becoming fatigued is more important than ever. It will be worth it because the real estate market in the greater Phoenix area is strong, with people migrating to escape ice and snow to the dry desert heat.

Chapter Eleven

LIVING TODAY AND LOOKING FORWARD

I live my life with very few regrets. I treasure and care for the beautiful people in my life. I intend to lead with love and keep a clear conscience by always trying to stay on the side of what's right. The adoption of this principle has created meaningful connections and long-lasting relationships for me. My every decision and deed is a brushstroke on my life's canvas, working toward a masterpiece of a well-lived life. Love gives me the strength to overcome challenges and the humility to enjoy my joy. It's my anchor amidst the storm and my compass in unknown waters. My relationships with family, friends, and strangers are more than just links; they are the threads that structure my tangled identity.

Taking care of my loved ones is a privilege and a responsibility. The true richness of life is shown in our shared laughter, silent understanding, and our unwavering support of each other in difficult times. The unique colors they bring to the mosaic of events make the adventure more vibrant and meaningful.

Leading with love requires a conscious choice to show compassion, kindness, and empathy in every interaction. It requires empathy and forgiveness for wrongdoers, even when things go wrong. This approach has formed my personality and my impact on the world.

Good behavior drives my moral choices. Accomplishing such demands requires honesty and doing justice to your relationships. Justice can be challenging, but it guarantees that my conscience will always be clear and that my actions will be in accordance with my values.

I find comfort in knowing that my journey is purposeful and honest as I navigate life's challenges. Living with few regrets implies one has learned a lot, not that one has made no mistakes. I live by love and righteousness, seeing each day as an opportunity to improve the world and leave a legacy of kindness and compassion. There is freedom in living a truthful, authentic life. I'm not perfect, but I try to steadily improve.

Having said that, if I could go back to my younger days, I would have taken the time to learn about managing my health better to prevent illness. Physical, mental, and spiritual wellness.

I'm a well-educated person with my undergraduate and master's degrees who just didn't really focus on my health until I had to. I took it for granted, which thankfully didn't prove to be a fatal mistake it could have been.

I didn't know processed foods like pre-packaged lunch meats have a shelf life of a few weeks, compared to fresh-cut deli ham or turkey with a five-day life, free of preservatives. We won't even get into the longevity of pre-packaged, cellophane-wrapped desserts. Years! And I used to love that stuff, along with a meal of BBQ pork with sides and sauces from a place in downtown Brooklyn.

While I realize what things can happen to even the most physically fit person, I believe if you stay on top of healthy habits and wellness from a young age, an active, longer, vibrant life is more likely. It's as basic as maintaining your car that you'd like to keep to its maximum mileage. It's maintaining the mechanical, plumbing, electrical, and brain of the car, with your health being a lot more important.

Investment in your health is like routine maintenance on a high-performance car. Like caring for a car's engine, brakes, and electrical system, we must care for our bodies. Consistent exercise, a good diet, mental health therapy, and enough sleep keep our bodies' complex machinery running smoothly. Building excellent habits early on is like laying a solid foundation. Our youth decisions affect our health throughout our lives. Regular exercise and a healthy diet have the potential to extend and improve our lives. This is like how oil changes and inspections extend the car's life.

The brain is a sophisticated mechanism, just like a car. Mental health is crucial, and regular cognitive exercises, stress management, and pleasant relationships are like fine-tuning a car's complex computer systems. Well-maintained brains improve cognitive performance and emotional capability. Our bodies wear out like any other car used frequently as we age. Regular healthcare is needed and may lessen wear and tear over time. Like frequent inspections, they identify possible issues before they even worsen.

Thinking of our bodies as highly tuned machines motivates us to take charge of our health. Just like a well-maintained car can last for years, taking care of our physical and mental health can elongate our lives.

As an Iraq war veteran, I have an appreciation for the basics and keeping life simple. I also learned how to do more with less by problem-solving and being resourceful. This is because serving in the military gave me the mental strength that I didn't know I lacked.

We hear about others getting cancer or having a heart attack or stroke, and it's our nature to think, *"It won't happen to me."*

Without self-care, it 'will' happen to any or all of us. Mindful food and beverage consumption, regular exercise that's right for you, and cultivating a strong mind go a long way in putting a health crisis prevention plan in place.

I'm grateful I never developed the habit of smoking. Beyond the increased risks of developing lung cancer, I learned that prolonged smoking causes damage to the heart and blood vessels leading to it. Tobacco use and too much alcohol raise blood pressure.

Over time, I've grown to appreciate my decision to never smoke. Smoking causes a variety of health problems, including lung cancer. Tobacco smoke contains substances that damage the cardiovascular system, causing artery constriction and hardness. Because of this, the heart must work harder to pump blood throughout the body. By avoiding this behavior, I've reduced my risk of lung and heart disease.

To make matters worse, understanding how smoking and alcohol affect blood pressure is crucial for us. Smoking and heavy drinking raise blood pressure, straining the heart and increasing the risk of cardiovascular disease and stroke. I've helped maintain good blood pressure by avoiding these risky activities and making research-based judgments. My cardiovascular system is less stressed for now.

This explains that our lifestyle choices affect health. Abstaining from smoking and limiting alcohol usage are investments in a healthy, long-lived future. Gratitude for these healthy habits inspires ongoing decisions, establishing the groundwork for a heart-healthy and rewarding existence.

Prevention.... Prevention... Prevention... by knowing your risk factors.

I don't proclaim to know everything. I'm a normal guy who loves his wife. My hope is I can help others by sharing my story, such that my mistakes are instrumental in preventing yours. Once I recognized what led to my illness, my drive to be free of it became stronger. I want this for everyone who can empathize with my long, tedious road to stroke recovery.

Spirituality and my faith saw me through my moments of darkness and despair more than once. Most of our religion is grounded in 'goodness', to live life with a compassionate heart and serve humanity. Exploring and choosing your religion or spiritual path is personal, but it's also incredibly important to your overall well-being.

Human nature is to place a label on your faith. I say, lean into your beliefs and respect the differences in others as long as they, too, are grounded in kindness. The purpose of religion is to wrap ourselves in as much goodness as possible while throwing a suffocating blanket on negativity and evil.

The range of beliefs held worldwide shows the depth of our collective experience. It's reasonable to look for a framework to understand and deepen our faith, but the most important thing to look for is our principles. Embracing one's convictions and finding inner peace through spirituality may be powerful and meaningful. However, it is crucial to recognize that people experience love, compassion, and kindness differently.

Recognizing and accepting different ideas helps create a peaceful environment. Faith's main goal is to uplift the human spirit by harboring relationships and understanding, not division. When turned into love, religious or spiritual differences can strengthen communities.

Religion is a moral compass that encourages kindness and protects us from evil. Rituals, teachings, and traditions promote virtue and discourage malice to improve society. We can shield ourselves against hatred and wickedness by surrounding ourselves with positive values.

We are united by our goodwill in a diverse society. The pursuit of morality unites all faiths, regardless of label. The ultimate measure of our ideas' value is their positive impact on our actions and the world around us as we navigate the complex tapestry of religious and spiritual variety. Keep this in mind as we negotiate this complicated concept. Thus, let us embrace love, understanding, and empathy and throw off the suffocating blanket of negativity and evil that divides us.

Each of us has an instinctual desire to be happy and avoid suffering. No one in their right mind chooses pain – physical or emotional. Understanding what happened to me and why it happened fueled my strength and confidence to overcome the consequences of my stroke. It was the search for mental health that drove my body to overcome its malfunction. When you find yourself taken to the floor and unable to get up, there's really nothing more liberating than to find the inner power to fight fiercely for your future self.

My fight showed me that living, creating experiences, and spending time with those I love are more valuable than any attachment to possessions. Hardship clarifies life's values, showing that our existence is defined by the depth of our connections and the moments we share. As I faced challenges, I realized that possessions are unnecessary. Laughter with friends and family and hugs from loved ones throughout good times and bad are what matter most. The significance of these lifelong experiences is unmatched by material possessions.

Adversity highlights time's transience. By doing so, we learn to appreciate the present, enjoy the moment, and recognize the unique value of those who enrich our lives. Our possessions may pass, but our memories of loved ones will stay forever.

Knowing that life is greater than its material aspects gives people and the world freedom. When freed from undue attachment to possessions, one can travel anywhere with a lighter heart and clearer perspective. Finding meaningful connections and experiences takes precedence, which deepens one's understanding of living.

I returned from my conflict with battle wounds and a deep appreciation for life's intangibles. I knew I would always carry these wounds. Relationships, experiences, and love became true indicators of wealth. Through this newfound understanding, I realized that our hearts hold the most valuable belongings, not our hands. These experiences, people, and lasting ties make life special.

There are thousands of experiences I want to have before my body decides it's time to lie down and rest for good. I don't want to let life's rewards pass me by, so any time I think or say, "I wish we could do this..." or "That is going on my bucket list..." I write it down and then examine the barriers to why I'm not doing it. If it's time, then we pick a time. If it's money, then start saving. The idea of looking forward to experiences excites me.

I'm going to share some secrets with you:

- Any time you feel alone, whether it's isolation from a global pandemic or feeling like you're alone in your health struggles, remember that you're never alone. There are people all over the world who just want to be connected. It's important as humans that we embrace those who are struggling, disabled, or isolated with kindness and understanding. Whether we're able to physically stand side-by-side or we're connected through history, experiences, and memories at a distance, it's the visuals we can each pull up in our minds to see the people who love us to glean comfort.

- You are reading this, breathing, and living your life right now, today. And, tomorrow, today will be gone. Free yourself from the past. You can't undo what's already happened. Grow from it.

- I can't undo my stroke and what led up to it. It's great to have a vision of your future, but don't live for it by sacrificing today. Think about the empowerment to live more freely in the present.

- Cultivate a strong mind and heart by being open to conquering the 'impossibilities'. You need an open and resilient attitude to succeed in self-discovery and development. One must be willing to face hardship, challenge preconceived notions, and explore new ground to succeed in this pursuit. Remember, perceived boundaries are often self-imposed and can be transcended with perseverance. Recognizing this is necessary to overcome 'impossibilities'. Success requires seeing challenges as opportunities for personal growth rather than insurmountable obstacles. Openness to new ideas, opinions, and experiences is also crucial to a strong mind and heart. It allows people to adapt and resourcefully overcome challenges, making them more robust. Overcoming 'impossibilities' motivates the development of a growth mindset. Failures are opportunities to improve and learn, not everlasting losses. It involves self-reflection and a dedication to personal development to evolve and become the best version of yourself. Accepting "impossibilities" to build a strong mind and heart is a comprehensive approach to personal growth.

- Focus on what's right, not what's wrong. When you're coming back from physical, mental, or spiritual trauma, small victories will feed you and sustain you for more. They will grow like a tree in strength, beauty, and stature.
- With energy, belief, and determination, you have the power to overcome anything.
- When you're overwhelmed... take a deep breath and remember to eat the "elephant" that weighs you down one bite at a time so you don't choke.

Be your best self and keep your glass half full. My life was turned upside down when I had a stroke at the beginning of COVID lockdown when I was home alone. It was a horrible trifecta that typically would have been the end, based on the two days I laid on the floor before getting the care I needed.

I see life so differently now with gratitude for every breath in my body. I am not going to waste this gift of a second chance I've been given. Any time I think of being lazy or eating that fried basket of food, I quickly revert back to all I've gone through to fight my way back physically, cognitively, and spiritually. I stay away from those temptations that are self-defeating and give myself a daily gift of wellness without any feeling of being deprived. Deprived for me would be finding myself back in a bed, wheelchair, or walker.

Epilogue

My overriding purpose for writing this book is to share my story in hopes others will learn from it. I'm not a doctor or healthcare professional. I'm a middle-aged army veteran who proudly served our country for nearly two decades. I am a loving husband and family man, and honestly, a normal person just like you, who just didn't see "it" coming.

I've been given a new purpose in life that is grounded in a deep sense of gratitude for being alive. I pay attention to what's in front of me, not what rests behind me.

Whether it is God or whatever loving, positive higher power you believe in, I hope you can recognize the complexity and miracle of the human body and its workings. It is magnificent and interconnected. Your temple is to be maintained and never taken for granted.

About The Author

Alvis (affectionately known as 'Al' amongst family and friends) Smith served as a soldier with the United States Army for almost two decades. He served with the 82nd Airborne Division as a paratrooper; he was also part of the (RIP) Ranger Indoctrination Program. Al also did two tours in Iraq, receiving many accommodations and awards. He was stationed at Fort Bragg, North Carolina, Vincenza, Italy, and Fort Benning, Georgia. He was a platoon sergeant at Fort Benning and in Italy.

Al Smith is a tenacious, hardworking, goal oriented, self-determined professional real estate broker. His accomplishments in real estate are a result of his clearly defined goals. He spent 20 years as a real estate agent and a real estate broker in Georgia and New York. Al was a real estate broker at Coldwell Banker in New

Rochelle, after which he worked at Better Homes and Garden Rand Realty in the Bronx and in Yonkers.

In April of 2020, Al suffered a stroke, that impacted him both mentally and physically. He laid on the floor inside his Mamaroneck, New York apartment for two days before Clayton, his dear friend, contacted him and summoned emergency services and the paramedics.

ordeal public health virus
gloves changes panic
irritable isolation crisis
mental health bored staying home infection
changes inside boredom social
face mask exposure morale distancing
quarantine mask quarantined impact
loneliness depressed protests social distancing news
email lockdown policies prevention frustration
contact contagion enforcement no contact boredom
communicable CDC mandates sequester discouraged
cabin fever listless resentment restless distance restrictions
Coronavirus stay home LOCKDOWN out of touch
personal QUARANTINE stress hopelessness
despair protective equipment no gathering
desolation helpless healthy concern
PPE downhearted boring social media
COVID-19 healthcare no visiting dispirited
anxiety family isolation
difficult masks
worry
isolated anger
isolate fear
depression
fear

Printed in the United States
by Baker & Taylor Publisher Services

Printed in the United States
by Baker & Taylor Publisher Services